Rockin' Blues Licks

Learn from the Blues Greats Themselves

Dozens of Authentic Licks That Sound Great over Each Portion of the Blues Progression

by Dave Celentano

ISBN 978-1-60378-435-1

Visit our website at www.cherrylaneprint.com

Contents

Introduction 4
About the Author 5
Acknowledgments 5
Bars 1 and 2 6
    Volker Strifler 6
    Chris Cain 7
    Eric Clapton 8
    Alvin Lee 9
    Warren Haynes 10
    Muddy Waters 11
    Buddy Guy 12
    Jonny Lang 13
    Jeff Beck 14
Bars 3 and 4 15
    Volker Strifler 15
    Chris Cain 16
    Warren Haynes 17
    Jeff Beck 18
    Rick Derringer 19
    Johnny Winter 20
    Richie Sambora 21
Bars 5 and 6 22
    Volker Strifler 22
    Chris Cain 23
    Eric Clapton 24
    Warren Haynes 25
    Muddy Waters 26
    Jeff Beck 27
    Johnny Winter 28
    Richie Sambora 29
    Mark Karan 30
    Keith Richards 31
Bars 7 and 8 32
    Volker Strifler 32
    Chris Cain 33
    Warren Haynes 34
    Jeff Beck 35
    Johnny Winter 36

Bars 9 and 10..37

    Volker Strifler 37

    Chris Cain 38

    Eric Clapton 39

    Alvin Lee...40

    Warren Haynes 41

    Jeff Beck 42

    Johnny Winter 43

    Mark Karan 44

    Jerry Garcia 45

Bars 11 and 12 46

    Volker Strifler 46

    Chris Cain 47

    Eric Clapton 48

    Muddy Waters 49

    Jeff Beck 50

    Johnny Winter 51

    Mark Karan 52

Backing Tracks 53

    Fast Tempo Backing Track 53

    Medium Tempo Backing Track 54

    Slow Tempo Backing Track 55

Introduction

Featuring examples from 15 legendary guitarists, this book presents blues guitar in a unique and fun way by deconstructing the classic 12-bar form into six easy-to-digest two-bar chunks. Each two-bar section features several examples; this approach makes comparing an idea over the first two measures a delight (for example, comparing the riffs of Muddy Waters with those of Buddy Guy, Jeff Beck, or Eric Clapton). All the examples are in the key of A and are played over one of three different backing tracks—slow, medium, or fast tempo—with all three tempos represented in each section. Learning two bars at a time allows you to observe how each phrase works over its corresponding chord(s) at a comfortable pace. Since the six sections contain many hip examples, a new solo can be constructed by connecting a favorite lick from each section. Feel free to mix and match; with tools of this quality, you can't go wrong.

While I strongly encourage you to work through this entire book, you can also use it as a reference guide for blues ideas. For instance, you may be looking for some fresh turnaround ideas, or perhaps new ways to navigate the I-IV chords, or maybe you're just after some fiery Johnny Winter licks. It's all here, just waiting to be tapped into. In addition, the three accompanying backing tracks should not only be used for practicing these new ideas, but for you to jam over and rehearse your own blues inspirations. There are a lot of licks here, so grab your favorite guitar and let's get started!

Note: Track 1 contains tuning pitches.

About the Author

Dave Celentano is a freelance guitarist, music transcriber, composer, author, and educator living in southern California. After graduating from G.I.T. at Musician's Institute, he began writing educational guitar books, transcription books, videos, and DVDs for Centerstream Publications, Star Licks, Hal Leonard Corp., Music Sales, and Cherry Lane Music, and since then he's written numerous other publications. Dave was a part of legendary German guitarist Michael Schenker's first educational DVD, *The Legendary Guitar of Michael Schenker*, providing the instructional content, and transcribing Michael's licks. Dave has released two solo CDs, *Guitar Stew* and *Wicked Music Box*, and one with his former band Sir Real, *Johari's Window*, all available through his web site www.davecelentano.com. Some of his work with Cherry Lane Music includes the DVD *Mastering the Modes for Rock Guitar*, and recording the audio CD companions for the books *Stylistic History of Heavy Metal*, *Joe Satriani's Guitar Secrets*, and *Guitar Secrets*.

Acknowledgments

Much thanks goes out to Cherry Lane's top dog John Stix and editor Mark Phillips, who together made this book possible. Also, extra special thanks to my family and the many awesome teachers and mentors I've had.

– *Dave Celentano*

Bars 1 and 2

Volker Strifler

over fast tempo backing track

Originally raised in Germany and currently based in Northern California, Volker Strifler is a remarkably talented musician who wears several hats, including guitarist, singer, songwriter, and producer. Although primarily a blues guitarist, his attraction to jazz (Wes Montgomery and Dave Brubeck are among his influences) surely helped to inform the chromaticism sprinkled throughout this fiery example. Chromatic notes tend to smooth out the otherwise angular sound of the straight blues-type scale.

TRACK 02 **TRACK 03**
Slow Demo

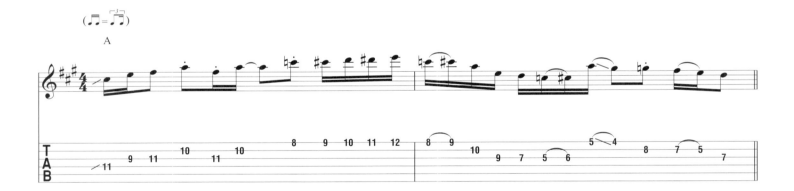

Rockin' Blues Riffs

Chris Cain

over fast tempo backing track

Unlike the Strat-wielding Stevie Ray Vaughan wannabies, Chris Cain's meaty Gibson tone (most often a Gibson 335) drives his "Three Kings" guitar sound, while his warm and husky B.B. King–style vocals deliver the message. His formative years were spent listening to and learning from the recordings of blues giants including Albert King, Albert Collins, and B.B. King. Eager to expand his musical pallet, he studied music at San Jose City College where he eventually taught jazz improvisation classes. Cain, along with fellow bluesman Volker Strifler, recorded with the Ford Blues Band for the CD *In Memory of Michael Bloomfield*, a tribute to the late blues guitarist from Chicago. Contrary to the dense soloing of Strifler, Cain grabs from the less-is-more bag for this example, where the notes and rests are of about equal value. Dig how Chris nails the A tonality with a pair of half step bends to C♯ (the major 3rd of A). The challenge for some is to know when to ease off the gas pedal and not play. If you find yourself an offender, please consider the music maxim: silence is just as important as the notes in music.

TRACK 04

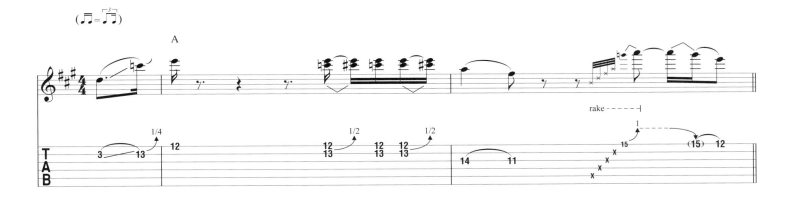

Eric Clapton

over fast tempo backing track

One of the most influential guitarists of our time and a name as ubiquitous as air, Eric Clapton (Slowhand, as his fans affectionately call him) has earned himself a position in rock and roll history. As an integral member of Cream, the Yardbirds, Blind Faith, John Mayall's Bluesbreakers, and Derek and the Dominos, he wrote and co-wrote many classic tunes and developed a killer guitar sound still sought after today by tone freaks. In fact, his performance on the album *John Mayall's Bluesbreakers with Eric Clapton* is regarded by many (Gary Moore and Joe Bonamassa to name a few) as the holy grail of guitar tones. In the following example, Clapton is anything but Slowhand! Here, he slams us with a two-beat idea that includes a whole step bend held in perfect tune while he plays a steady stream of 16th notes. This is repeated a second time to finish the bar, then is shortened by half to ramp up urgency before finally resolving. The strength and stability of your 3rd finger is tested here; therefore, reinforce the bend by placing the 2nd finger just behind the 3rd on the same string. Think of these two digits together as one big, fat bending finger.

TRACK 05 TRACK 06
Slow Demo

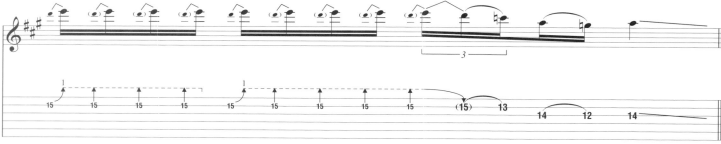

Alvin Lee

over fast tempo backing track

As one of the founding members of Ten Years After, Alvin Lee's performance at the original Woodstock festival was truly a highlight and is still referenced by guitarists today. If you don't believe it, check out his smoking display of chops on "I'm Going Home" from this historical concert. Although primarily a rock guitarist, his attraction to and prowess with the blues can't be overlooked. There's no subtlety in this example—it just burns, and is reminiscent of the rock-infused blues madness he laid upon the hippie ears at Woodstock. For an efficient way to pick the 16th note triplets, try using two downstrokes (a two string sweep) for the string crossing on the last two notes of each six-note grouping.

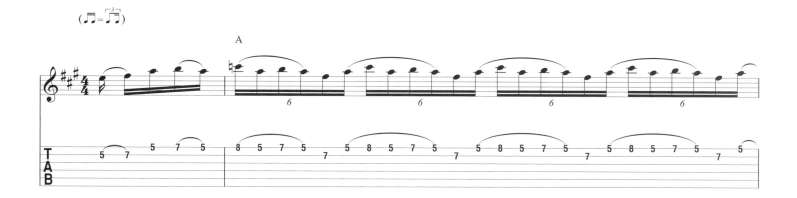

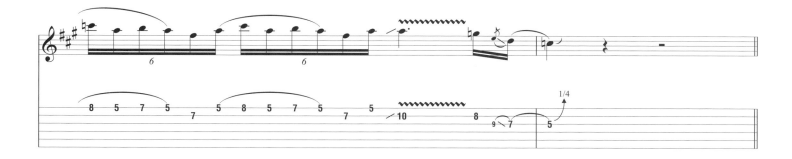

Warren Haynes

over medium tempo backing track

Warren Haynes is one busy musician! In addition to being a founding member of Gov't Mule, his stunning six-string fusion of rock, blues, R & B, and jazz has landed him long-standing positions in the Allman Brothers Band and the Grateful Dead. And if that's not enough, he regularly moonlights as a studio musician, recording or performing with an eclectic selection of musicians including Kid Rock, Eric Clapton, Bonnie Raitt, Dave Matthews, John Lee Hooker, and B.B. King. This 100 percent minor pentatonic example is a fantastic representation of Warren's phrasing. Here, he's building a dialog with his statements as he places space between the ideas, much like a saxophonist does as he catches breath between phrases.

TRACK 09

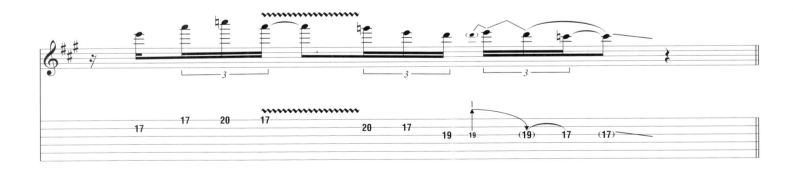

Muddy Waters

over medium tempo backing track

The Telecaster-slinging blues man Muddy "McKinley Morganfield" Waters is considered by many to be the father of modern Chicago blues and one of the first blues musicians to use (the now commonplace) drums, electric guitar, and bass as the core instrumentation for his band. Muddy had such and influence on musicians back in the day that the Rolling Stones even named themselves after one of his songs. For the following example, Muddy's stinging tone pierces through as he paraphrases himself by duplicating the first measure's idea again in the second measure. It cannot be overemphasized how important restating ideas (with or without slight variations) is to the blues genre. To meet blues approval, push those four B string quarter step bends just slightly sharp while holding the 1st string stationary. Dig the major 6th (F♯) added on top of the otherwise familiar minor pentatonic tones.

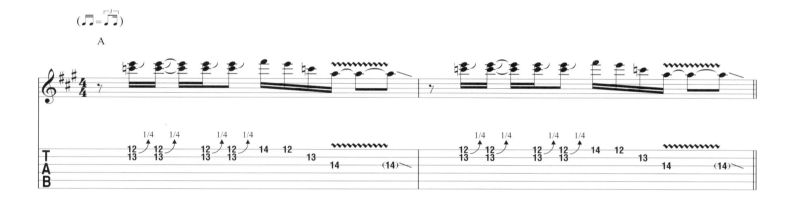

Buddy Guy

over medium tempo backing track

As a young man inspired by the blues sounds emanating from Chicago (Howlin' Wolf, Muddy Waters, and Little Walter in particular), Louisiana-born Buddy Guy hopped a train north to the Windy City to check it out firsthand. The influence that these big-time players had on young Buddy is evident in this example. For instance, the first bar finds him playing in the same territory and using similar note choices as the first bar of the Muddy Waters example. Instead of an oblique bend though (as Muddy did), Guy plays the quarter step bends on the B string separate from the E note on the 1st string. He even includes the hip-sounding F♯ (major 6th). The second bar captures the A7 tonality by including the juicy C♯ (major 3rd) and G (♭7th). Soloists should always be aware of the chord(s) they're playing over, and highlighting and/or ending on an individual chord tone makes for a convincing and melodic performance.

TRACK 11

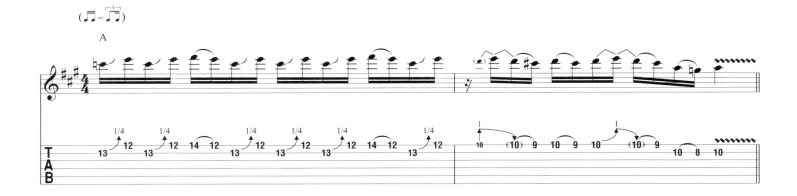

Jonny Lang

over medium tempo backing track

As the elder blues statesmen move on in life, the torch is being passed down; one of the recipients is the young blues singer and guitarist Jonny Lang. Beginning guitar at age 12, this North Dakota native released his first CD when he was only 14 and has since opened for many national acts, including the Rolling Stones, Buddy Guy, B.B. King, and Jeff Beck. In this burning minor pentatonic idea, Lang spits out 32nd notes that would rival most shred guitarists. Essentially, it's a four-note lick played twice per beat—the first begins on the "down" of the beat, and the second on the "and." By all means, learn the phrase and practice with a metronome to gradually build up speed.

TRACK 12 **TRACK 13**
Slow Demo

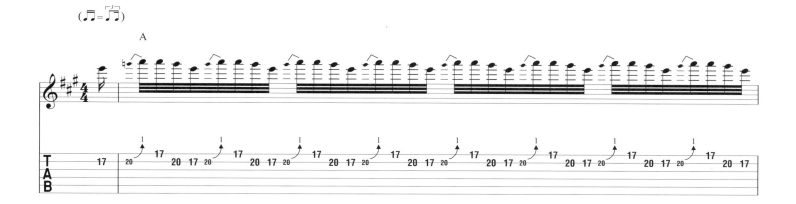

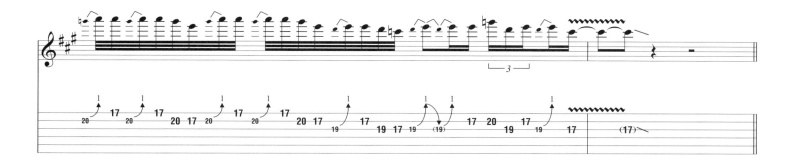

Jeff Beck

over slow tempo backing track

Not one to be pinned to a singular style, Jeff Beck has explored and conquered rock, fusion, and blues while stamping each with his own unique touch. A big part of Beck's sound comes from the way he plucks the strings; he eschews a pick in favor of fingers for producing a warmer tone. While some soloists choose to repeat an idea verbatim, here the pickless wonder establishes an idea on the first two beats, then bounces it down an octave for the second half of the bar. Whether duplicating a lick or stringing together separate ideas, all soloists worth their salt develop phrases that talk to each other in a call and response manner. This is often the measure of how well a soloist can create a conversational dialog and communicate it to the audience.

TRACK 14

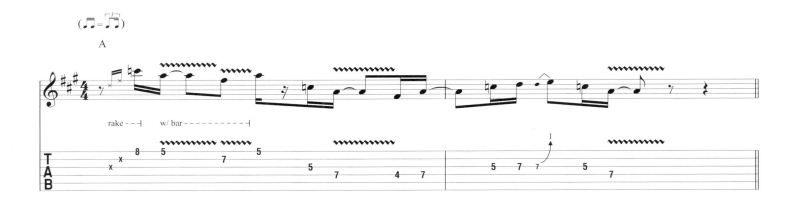

Bars 3 and 4

Volker Strifler

over fast tempo backing track

Whether Volker Strifler is playing with the Ford Blues Band, touring as a sideman for Robben Ford, or fronting his own group, he is a force to be reckoned with. The adage "less is more" is thrown out the door here as Strifler manages (in a tasty and melodic manner) to cram a steady stream of 16th notes into this two-bar phrase, which concludes with a double stop string bend hinting at the ensuing IV chord (D).

TRACK 15 TRACK 16
Slow Demo

Chris Cain

over fast tempo backing track

Cain's first of two ideas captures the major tonality by highlighting the major 3rd (C♯) with a repeated string-bending lick played over the A chord. Repetition in music is a powerful tool for building tension and is typically followed by a resolving idea. In this case, the bending lick resolves wonderfully on the A note in the last bar. His spot-on intonation and control at every bend sells this lick and makes it rock. More repetition is applied in the latter half of the second example as Chris repeats a three-note figure using a 16th note rhythm. This is similar to the hemiola technique of playing a rhythm pattern of three beats in the time of two, or vice versa. Notice how this produces a "floating above the beat" feel before resolving.

TRACK 17

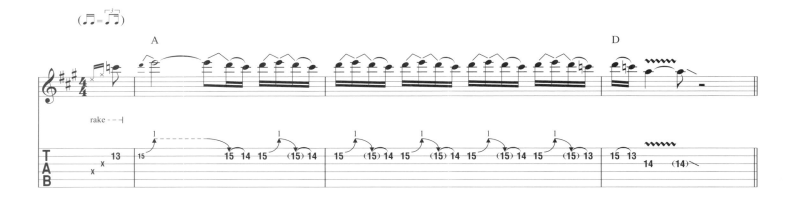

TRACK 18

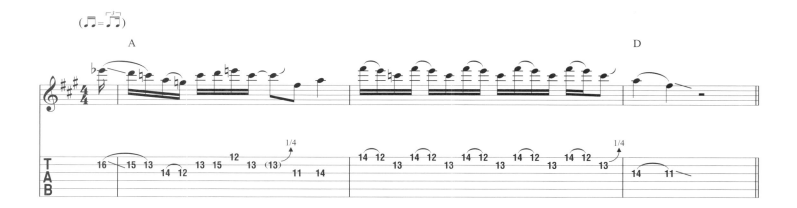

Warren Haynes

over medium tempo backing track

Some cool string bending and minor pentatonic usage going on here from Warren Haynes. It all starts with a gradual bend as he continuously picks 16th note triplets. The objective is to push the string slightly more sharp with each pick stroke until it reaches a whole step. Haynes is comfortable in any string bending situation, including the super-challenging reverse string bend using the index finger, shown on beat one and a half of the second bar. Here he pre-bends the string a whole step followed by pick and release. Try wrapping the left-hand thumb over the top edge of the neck for a better grip. Finally, check out the whole and half step bends near the end of the example, each tailed with a quick vibrato. Proper intonation is paramount, and any blues soloist must master the various bending techniques as a sort of rite of passage.

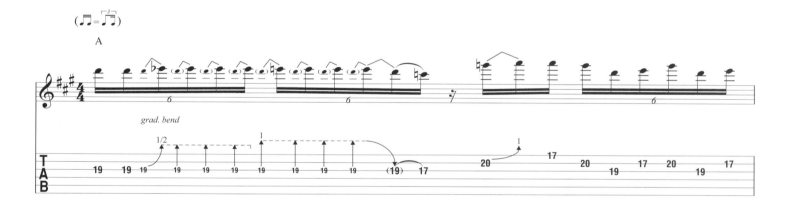

Jeff Beck

over slow tempo backing track

Beck's unique style includes lots of whammy bar usage and this laid-back example features a couple of tasty ideas. After the initial bend, grab the whammy bar and gently vibrato (shake) while holding the string in the bent position. Using the whammy with vibrato allows Jeff to gently move the target note slightly flat and sharp, resulting in a more vocal type of vibrato. At the end of the example, play the half step dips by quickly depressing and releasing the whammy bar.

TRACK 21

Rick Derringer

over medium tempo backing track

Although primarily a rock guitarist (his first band, the McCoys, had a No. 1 pop hit with "Hang On Sloopy" in 1965), Rick Derringer can dish out some delicious blues. Texas bluesman Johnny Winter even commissioned Rick to play on and produce several of his albums, including *Johnny Winter And*, *Live Johnny Winter And*, and *Still Alive and Well*. Like most skilled soloists, Rick uses the third and fourth measures to build excitement and anticipation of the approaching change to the IV chord. Using just the 1st and 3rd fingers and a few minor pentatonic boxes, he blows over the two-bar setup with a series of 16th note reverse bends, followed by accelerated sextuplets and 32nd notes before resolving on C (the ♭7th of the following D chord). The squeal-like tone on the reverse bends is the result of artificial harmonics (pinch harmonics), and is created when you strike the string with the side of the thumb along with the pick.

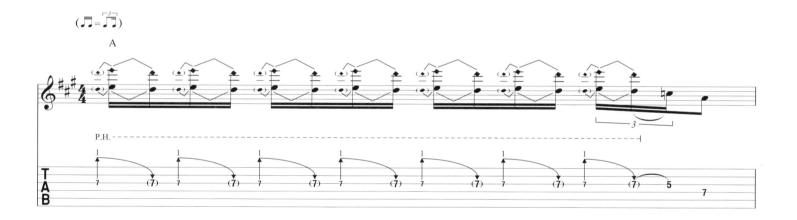

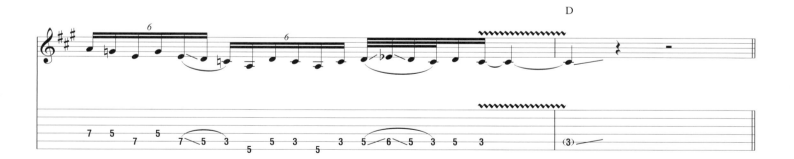

Johnny Winter

over medium tempo backing track

Johnny Winter's fiery Texas blues style is without equal. Considered the torchbearer for the blues during the '70s and early '80s, Winter carried the flag at a time when blues was not in style. During this period, an early incarnation of his band featured bassist Tommy Shannon, who would later join Stevie Ray Vaughan's Double Trouble. This smoking example rolls through the notes with a triplet feel using sextuplets (six notes per beat). In the second half, notice the greasy sliding lick incorporating the blue note (E♭) and 32nd notes, and how Rick Derringer played the same move (albeit one octave lower) for his example over the same two bars.

TRACK 24 **TRACK 25**
Slow Demo

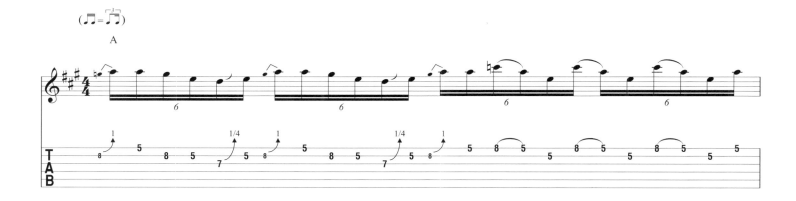

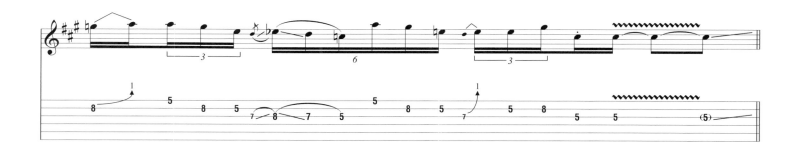

Richie Sambora

over medium tempo backing track

Primarily known as Bon Jovi's guitarist and songwriting partner, Richie Sambora pulls off a lively Dorian blues lick for this example. Staying with the A tonality, the dorian-blues scale is a hybrid scale that fuses notes of A Dorian (A, B, C, D, E, F♯, G) with A blues (A, C, D, E♭, E, G), resulting in A Dorian-blues (A, B, C, D, E♭, E, F♯, G). A huge benefit that this new scale presents is the repetitive patterns of the 5th, 7th, and 8th frets on the top three strings. With common fingerings like these, it's easy to fall back on repeating licks that are easily moved across the strings. Here, Richie refrains from this issue and puts stock in a musically interesting and fun-to-play phrase. For the second half, he takes a more simple and stripped-down approach using repeated double stops.

TRACK 26   TRACK 27
Slow Demo

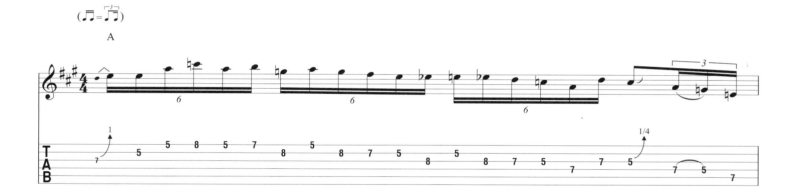

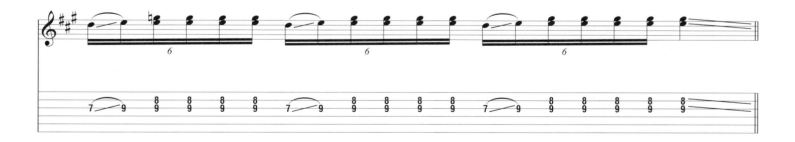

Bars 5 and 6

Volker Strifler

over fast tempo backing track

Here are two different approaches Strifler takes on the IV chord (D). The first features a repeated hot-rod string-bending lick punctuating the A note (the 5th of D) for one and a half measures. Using repetition, as in this example, is a great way to draw the listener in and build excitement in a solo. This is followed by a quick descending run through the blues scale, finally releasing tension. As a soloist, one should take note of the chord that's being played over as well as its subsequent chord tones, as these are good notes to accentuate and/or end on. The chord tones for D7 are D (root), F♯ (3rd), A (5th), and C (♭7th).

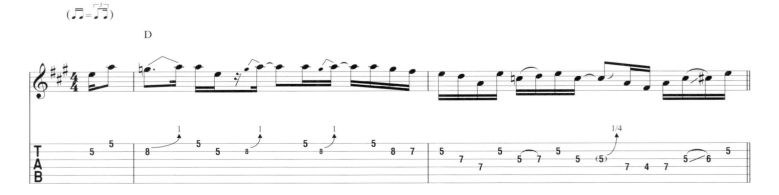

Chris Cain

over fast tempo backing track

Cain's command of the blues boxes and his effortless ease in shifting between them is displayed here in the first example. The first box, affectionately dubbed the "Albert King box," occurs on the first beat and a half, followed by the "B.B. King box" for the remainder of the bar. The final box utilizes a repeating motif that pronounces the underlying D chord perfectly by nailing F♯ (the 3rd) and C (the ♭7th). The second example features super cool string bending action right out of the B.B. King box. Here, the crazy bending happens in the second half of the example, which features a single whole step bend followed by a pair of two-step bends (ouch!). Practice these big bends by first playing the note four frets (two whole steps) above to give your ear the correct pitch, followed by much rehearsal bending up to this target pitch. For stability, you might find it easier to bend by gripping the string with two or more fingers before pushing upward. Also, try wrapping the left-hand thumb over the top of the neck (similar to gripping a baseball bat) for added support and leverage.

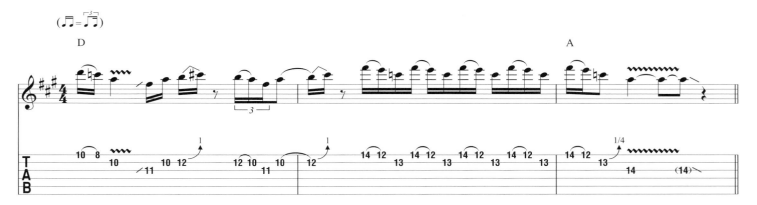

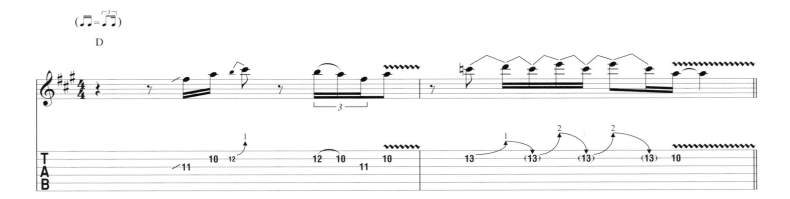

Eric Clapton

over fast tempo backing track

More detailed string bends here as Mr. Clapton demonstrates his spot-on intonation. All of the bending business is played over the D (IV) chord and is right out of the B.B. King box at the 10th fret. Watch the tricky bend in the last two beats of the example. Start by bending a whole step with the ring finger (also using the middle finger for added support), and hold in bent position while simultaneously fingering the 1st string with the pinkie. After three strikes on the pinkie note, re-pluck the bent string and release. These country-flavored oblique bends have become a mainstay in the blues and rock vocabulary, and, consequently, an important addition to the arsenal of all aspiring lead guitarists.

TRACK 35

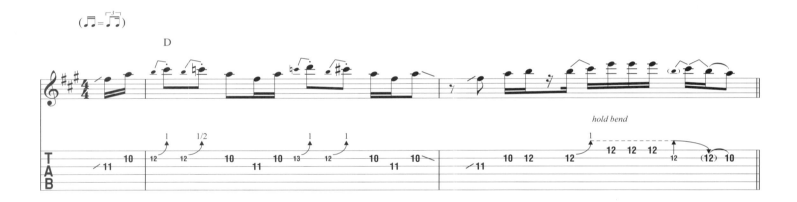

Warren Haynes

over slow tempo backing track

Interestingly, while most players opt to use the minor pentatonic during the IV chord, Haynes chooses major pentatonic—in this case A major pentatonic (A, B, C♯, E, F♯). This lazy idea drips and oozes major tonalities as he nails the D (IV) chord by hitting the chord tones—D (root), F♯ (3rd), and A (5th). Another great representation of major pentatonic usage like this occurs in the solo work of B.B. King; perhaps that's why soloing in the key of A in this area of the neck has become known as the "B.B. King box."

TRACK 36

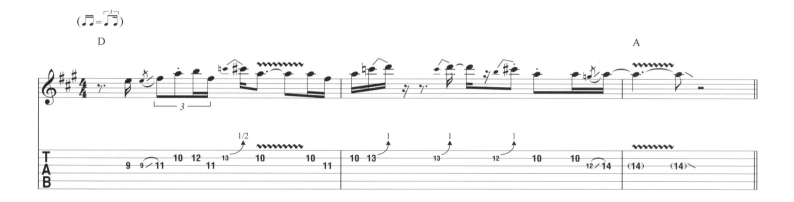

Muddy Waters

over medium tempo backing track

Here's a simple but effective idea that outlines the D (IV) chord. Beginning in the 10th position, Muddy captures most of the essential chord tones—F♯ (3rd), A (5th), and C (♭7th), before shifting to 5th position for the final slippery blues lick. Instead of duplicating the idea from bar 5 verbatim, he modifies the ending of the repeat in bar 6 to lead your ear to the ensuing A chord.

TRACK 37

Jeff Beck

over slow tempo backing track

Although the majority of notes from Beck's examples in this book are right out of A minor pentatonic (A, C, D, E, G), he tends to favor the F♯ (major 6th) instead of G (♭7). The inclusion of the 6th produces a slightly jazzier sound, and players like B. B. King and Eric Clapton have based their bluesy style around this note. Here, Jeff continues with more signature whammy bar subtleties, including gentle vibrato on held bent notes and a whammy bar dip. Dig the poppy tone he gets from plucking with his fingers. This is the result of the string snapping back against the frets as it's released from the plucking finger, similar to the slapping and popping of a funk bassist.

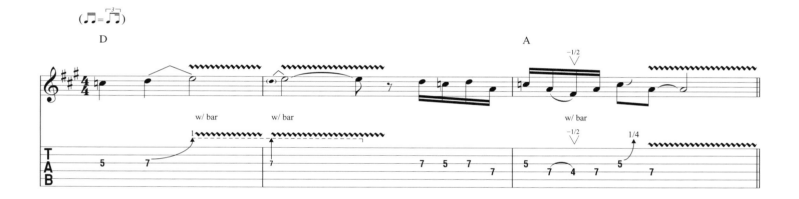

Johnny Winter

over medium tempo backing track

Here's a note-filled approach to the IV chord (D) from Mr. Winter. One of his many fortes includes the way he takes a simple pentatonic scale and makes it sound tasty. The first half is pure minor pentatonic, while the second is augmented with several appearances of the colorful and tension-yielding flatted 5th, which characterizes the blues scale.

TRACK 39   TRACK 40
Slow Demo

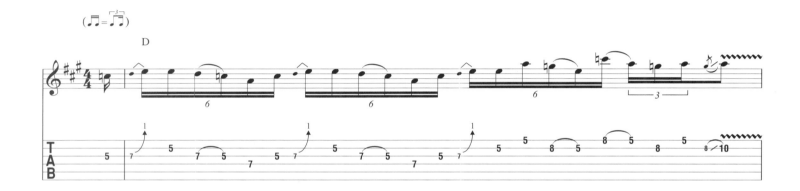

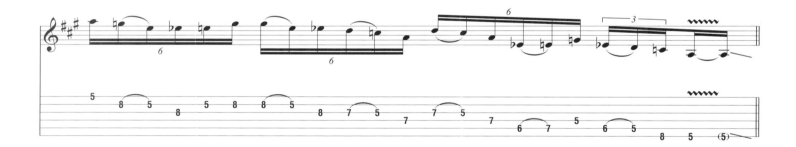

Richie Sambora

over medium tempo backing track

Here's a flashy example (complete with a few right-hand taps) of what a rock guitarist from the '80s might play over the bluesy IV chord (D). After the initial trill, Sambora proceeds to tap the 10th fret, 2nd string, with the edge of the pick and slides up the fretboard towards the bridge. As the pick reaches the end of the fretboard, it pulls off and generates the 5th fret note. Play the trill-tap-slide-pull-off sequence three times, then shift up to the 15th fret for a series of reverse bends followed by a short bluesy lick.

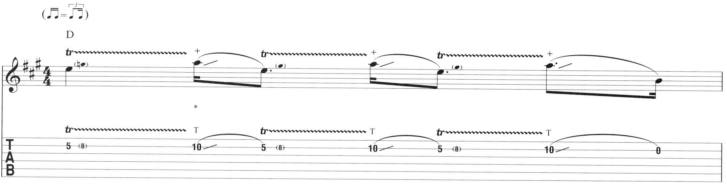

*Tap and slide up neck w/ edge of pick, then pull off to fretted notes.

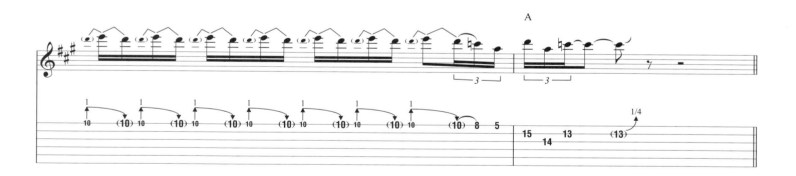

Mark Karan

over slow tempo backing track

A member of Grateful Dead alumnus Bob Weir's band Bob Weir and Rat Dog for over a decade, studio musician and producer Mark Karan is famous in the jam band circles as an inspired guitarist and soulful vocalist. The first half of the following example features speedy repetitions using an odd grouping of nine notes per beat. This should be felt as three groups of fast triplets per beat. Mark's rhythmic interpretation here demonstrates how flexible the timing issues are over a slow blues. The latter half showcases several string bending techniques, including a gradual bend where the string is pushed slightly more sharp with each subsequent pick strike.

TRACK 43 **TRACK 44**
Slow Demo

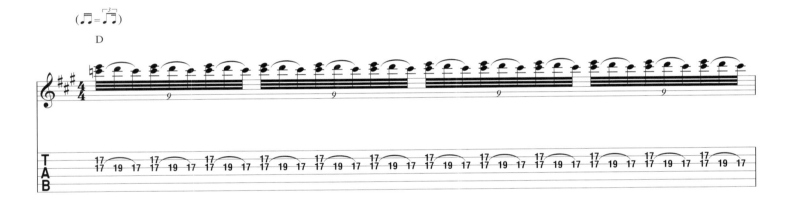

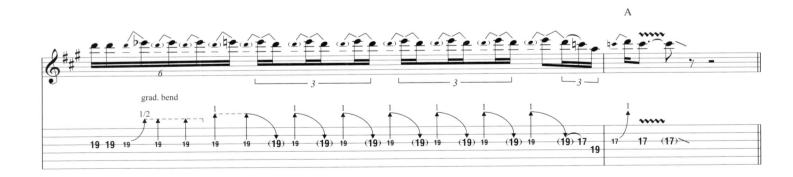

Keith Richards

over medium tempo backing track

One of Keith Richards' big influences is Chuck Berry, and this example drips with that '50s vibe. The old school double stops in conjunction with Keith's impeccable sense of syncopation and timing create a cool push and pull feel that's hard to beat. Also check out the call and response action going on between the two halves of the example, where the second half seems to reply back to the first. Use two fingers (ring and pinkie) rather than a barre for all of the double stop bends, as doing so affords more strength and control over each string.

TRACK 45

Bars 7 and 8

Volker Strifler

over fast tempo backing track

Similar to how the third and fourth bars function in the blues, bars seven and eight are used as a set up for the next two measures, anticipating the V and IV chords that follow. Check out Strifler's two contrasting ideas played over A (the I chord). The first features more fast licks and a touch of chromaticism thrown in to spice up the stew. Notice how the major/minor tonalities are tastefully blurred by including both the major and minor 3rds (C♯ and C, respectively). How well a guitarist can navigate between the two is a true test of his ability to make colorful and musical statements. Meanwhile, the majority of the second example consists of punchy double stops played with a mostly eighth note rhythm, with still another example of chromaticism at the tail end of the example, which smoothly guides the ear to the V chord (in this case E) of measure nine.

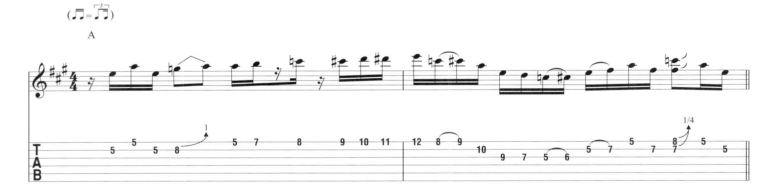

Chris Cain

over fast tempo backing track

Practitioners from the school of B.B. King will notice the ultra-cool and somewhat jazzy inclusion of the major 6th (F♯) sprinkled throughout the first example. Although not a chord tone from the implied A7 chord, the 6th can also be regarded as the 13th (the 6th bumped up one octave), which is an acceptable chord extension of A7. Extensions like the 13th and especially the 9th are quite commonplace and add wonderful color and dimension to the chords. Dig how Cain uses contrast here—an important composing and improvising tool—with loads of string bending action in the first half, juxtaposed with a jam-packed flurry of 16th notes in the latter. In the second example, he continues using more trademark devices including repetition, string bends, minor pentatonic activity, and another inclusion of the major 6th. The last note of the phrase (B) can be analyzed as the 5th of E (the next chord in the progression), and viewed as a lead-in for the following measure.

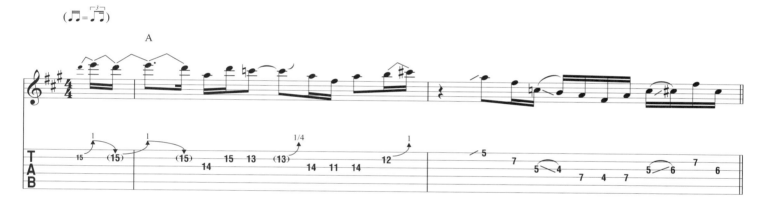

Warren Haynes

over slow tempo backing track

Here we find Haynes returning to the minor pentatonic with some greasy blues licks over the A chord for bars seven and eight (he just came from the D chord where he played predominantly A major pentatonic). Also, dig the over-bending in beat 3 of the first bar, where he bends up one and a half steps from E to G before a short descending idea using notes from A blues scale (A, C, D, Eb, E, G). Use two or more fingers for additional support and strength on big bends; plant the middle and index fingers just behind the ring finger (the primary bending finger).

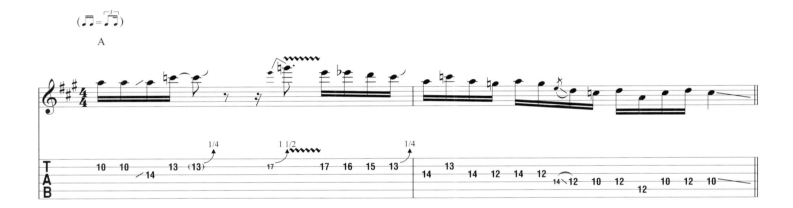

Jeff Beck

over slow tempo backing track

Here, Beck serves up a healthy dose of whammy bar using a new technique: whammy bar scoops. What's interesting is that this lick starts off by simply hammering on and pulling off (you won't pick anything with the right hand) while simultaneously and quickly depressing and releasing the whammy bar on selected notes for the scooping sound. The last part of the lick does an excellent job of directing our ear towards the approaching E7♯9 chord in measure nine by including the chord tones B and G (respectively the 5th and ♯9 of E7♯9).

TRACK 54

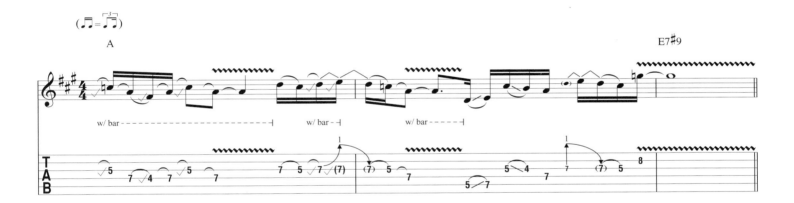

Johnny Winter

over medium tempo backing track

When it comes to soloing, variety can be a beautiful thing, as it keeps the listener interested. Here, Johnny shuns the jam-packed sextuplet recipe (used in bars 5 and 6) and takes a different approach by slowing down and leaving more space between notes. After the initial slide on the B string (which is a delight to play and gets everyone's attention), he positions himself at the 10th fret for a series of notes framing the bend and release. This is followed by a quick shift to the 5th fret for the wrap-up.

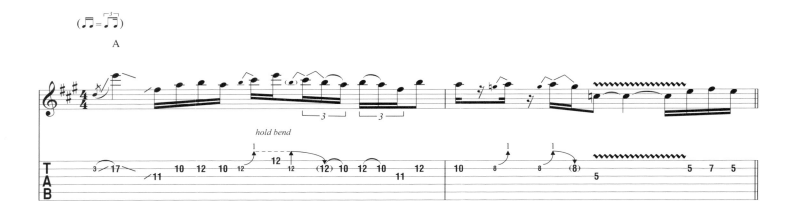

Bars 9 and 10

Volker Strifler

over fast tempo backing track

Bars 9 and 10 anticipate the turnaround, which occurs in bars 11 and 12. The first of two Strifler licks uses double and triple stops in a chromatic manner over the E (V) chord, while the D (IV) chord continues building excitement with a dense barrage of 16th notes. The second idea features a steady storm of notes that incorporates blues and jazz flavors. Here, Volker uses minor pentatonic exclusively for the first three quarters of the phrase, then gets jazzy for the final quarter by throwing in a few "outside notes." Generally, these outside notes are considered wrong choices in themselves, but when used sparingly, as in this example, they can be a very effective tool for connecting more acceptable notes.

Slow Demo

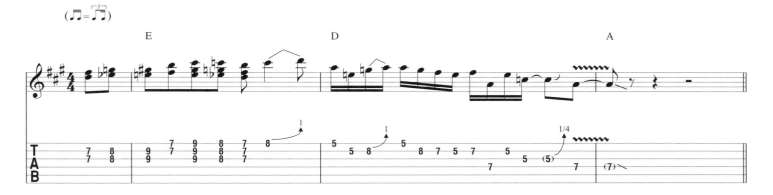

Slow Demo

Chris Cain

over fast tempo backing track

In the first of two ideas here, Chris blasts off with a quick burst of notes mostly using the A blues scale (A, C, D, E♭, E, G) before ending on D (the ♭7 of the E chord). The latter half employs almost all double stops played over the D chord and hits superbly on chord tones and extensions—D (root), F♯ (3rd), A (5th), C (♭7th), and E (9th). In the second example, Cain reveals more of his jazzy influences by acknowledging each chord with a separate scale. During the E chord he temporarily abandons the parent key of A and chooses to play the E blues scale (E, G, A, B♭, B, D) up to beat 3, where he finishes with a jazzy line including a touch of chromaticism. Next, the D chord is treated with a dose of D Mixolydian (D, E, F♯, G, A, B, C) and even hints at the upcoming A chord by including the C♯ note in the fourth beat.

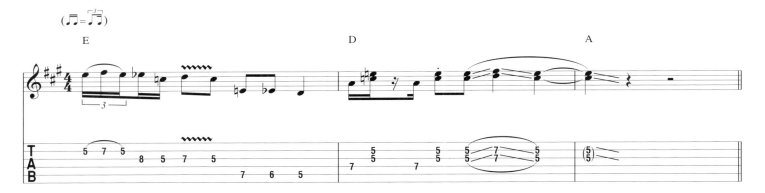

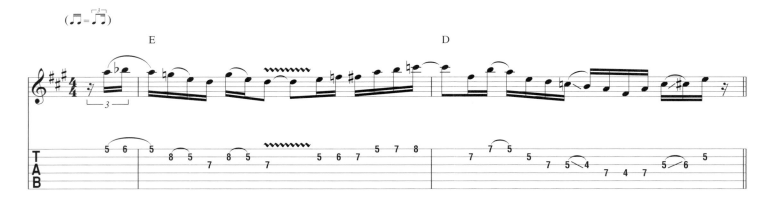

Eric Clapton

over fast tempo backing track

This lick from Eric Clapton features a variety of bending techniques, including whole and quarter step bends, a half step pre-bend and release (bend the string upward first, then pick and release) followed by a pull-off, and a whole step bend and release followed by a pull-off. It's been reported that Clapton strings his electric guitars with ultra-lights, so if all this string bending business proves to be a strain on your hand and fingers, perhaps you too will find more comfort and ease by stepping down to lighter gauge strings.

TRACK 64 **TRACK 65**
Slow Demo

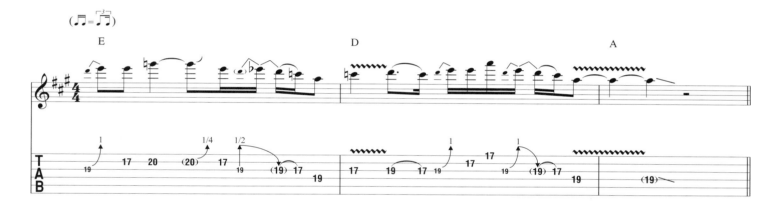

Alvin Lee

over fast tempo backing track

More killing and deceptively simple licks as Alvin Lee keeps the pedal to the metal and plays a repeating three-note pull-off lick over the E (V) chord. Although the lick contains only one chord tone (B—the 5th), Lee makes it sound delicious. Next, he moves the entire lick up three frets before resolving the phrase in the Albert King box for the A chord.

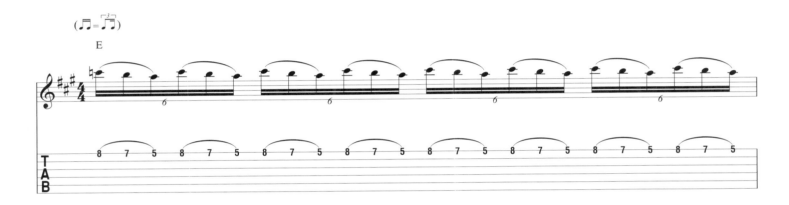

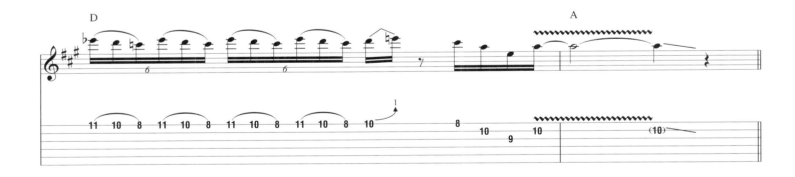

Warren Haynes

over medium tempo backing track

Intervals are an essential component of composing and soloing in many genres, including the blues. Basically, the expanse between any two notes is given a numeric name (2nd, 3rd, 4th, etc.), determined by the distance between them. Here, Warren offers up a delicious idea constituting a major 6th interval that pivots between the notes D and B. Playing intensely is a part of blues soloing, so don't be afraid to add vigorous vibrato to those four A notes on the high E string.

TRACK 68   **TRACK 69**
              Slow Demo

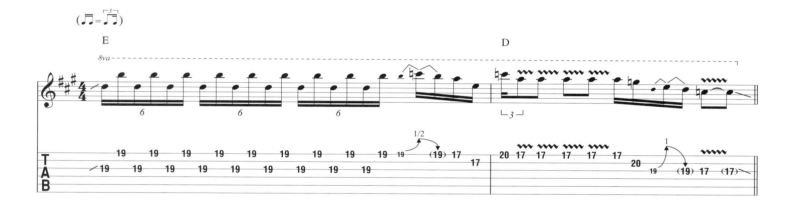

Jeff Beck

over slow tempo backing track

For the turnaround, Beck plays a psychedelic and non-traditional lick using the whammy bar. The first half of this example is a two-note idea, where the first pitch is pulled off to the second and then followed by a slow depression of the whammy bar. This is repeated, approximately, as he moves the idea across three strings from B down to D. The conclusion is a pure minor pentatonic dance on the 5th string that features a pair of quarter step bends executed with the index finger before resolving on A.

TRACK 70

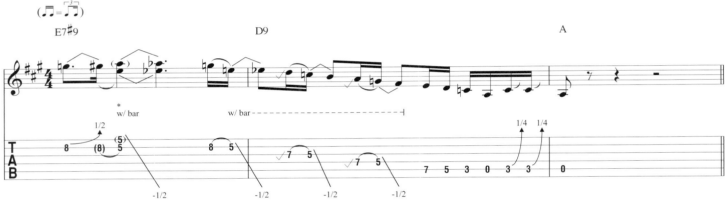

Johnny Winter

over medium tempo backing track

The turnaround is met with bends of many sorts as Winter begins by outlining the V chord (E) with chord tones (E, G♯ and B) using a sustained bend, reverse bend to pull-off, and full bend. For the D chord, he moves up to 12th position with a series of unison bends followed by a reverse bend, which resolves to the A note. String bending techniques like these produce a beautiful vocal quality and allow the notes to breath and resonate—something that is absent in a solo crammed with notes. The goal of a soloist is to find a balance between active and restrained passages.

TRACK 71

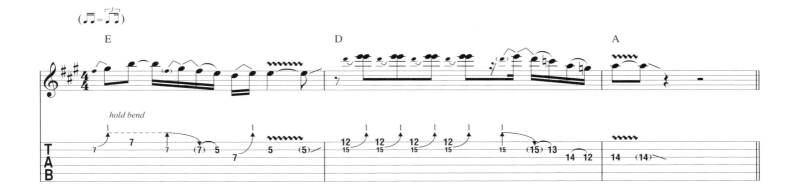

Mark Karan

over slow tempo backing track

Mark nails the changes wonderfully in this lick, where he begins by temporarily applying the E blues scale (E, G, A, B♭, B, D) during the E7♯9 (V) chord, a move often associated with T-Bone Walker and Stevie Ray Vaughan. For the D9 (IV) chord, Karan alternates between two chord tones, F♯ and A (the 3rd and 5th of D9, respectively), before ending with a pair of two-whole-step bends from C to E (the ♭7th and 9th of D9, respectively). Sweet!

TRACK 72

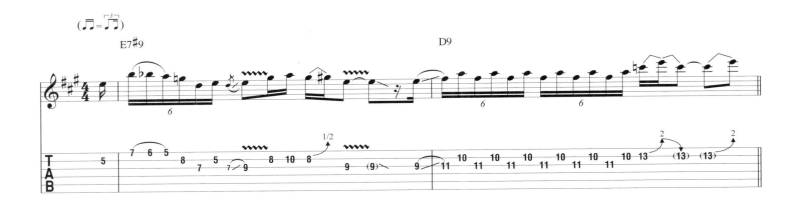

Jerry Garcia

over slow tempo backing track

As a member of the Grateful Dead and one of the forefathers of the jam band genre (before "jam band" was a term), Jerry Garcia's improvisational work is full of surprises. For this hip, imaginative lick, Jerry's note choice is unpredictable yet melodic. The idea bounces and bends its way along, hitting several strategic chord tones along the path. You'll need to use the unsupported index finger for the last three bends, a practice often avoided but one that should be mastered nevertheless.

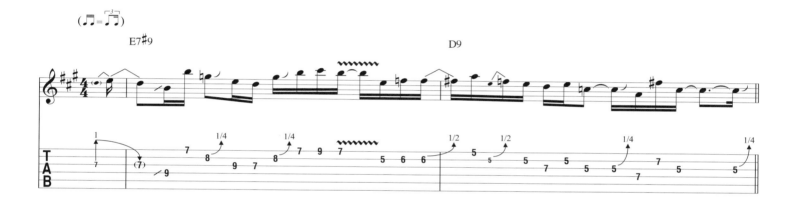

Bars 11 and 12

Volker Strifler

over fast tempo backing track

And at last the conclusion. When the solo is coming to an end, most soloists use the last two measures as a wrap-up, to give a sense of closure to the solo. One of two things usually happens here: the soloist will ease up and bring the solo down gracefully to its conclusion, or, in what's known as a *turnaround*, he'll ramp up the intensity with a phrase that leads into another 12-bar solo. For the first example, Volker chooses the former and reveals his country influences by adhering strictly to major pentatonic. Use the 1st and 3rd fingers exclusively to perform this lick and notice the shift between pentatonic boxes. In the second example, he raises the energy level making this jam-packed and jumpy line seem like a walk in the park. You would be wise to take this one slow at first, as the sheer number of notes and string skips could present a challenge.

TRACK 74   TRACK 75
Slow Demo

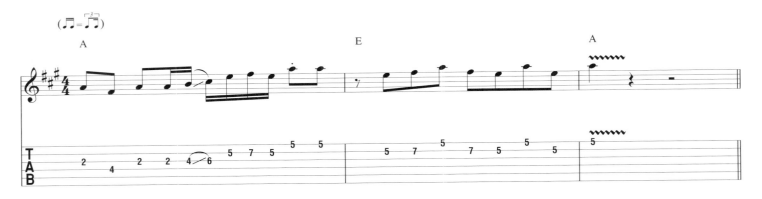

TRACK 76   TRACK 77
Slow Demo

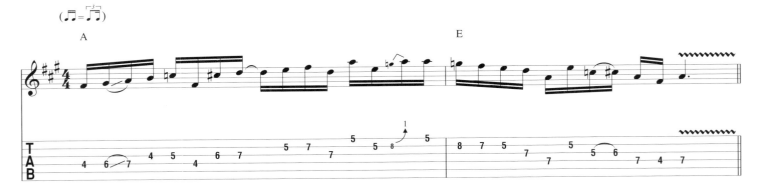

Rockin' Blues Riffs

Chris Cain

over fast tempo backing track

At this point, Mr. Cain eases off the gas pedal slightly with a slow and spacious bend during the first three beats, then concludes with a Clapton-esque run (think Cream's live version of "Crossroads") ascending an A major triad (A, C♯, E). Although the underlying chord here is E (V chord), he gains acceptance for the A triad by concluding with a pair of punchy E notes to capture the V chord. For the second idea, Cain plays a line contrary to the first, which ended with an ascending motion. Here, the line generally unfolds in a descending order. Watch out for the beginning, which leads off with a whole step bend followed by a half step bend. Proper intonation for string bending can be elusive and should be rehearsed until definitive results are achieved.

TRACK 78

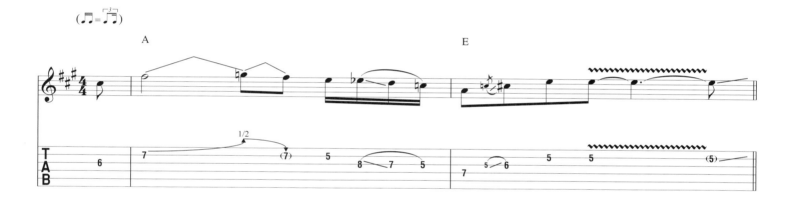

TRACK 79

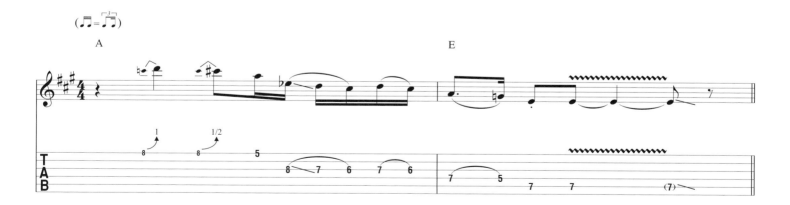

Eric Clapton

over fast tempo backing track

Always aware of the chords he solos over, Clapton navigates the blues changes with confidence and ease, and the turnaround is no exception. Here, Eric winds things down and brings the turnaround to a magnificent close as he plays a pure A minor pentatonic scale (A, C, D, E, G) over the A chord before tagging the C♯ (the major 3rd of A) at the start of the last measure. From this point he works his way down an A major triad before concluding on the root of the E (V) chord.

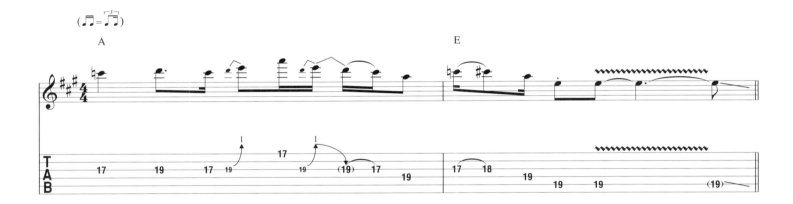

Muddy Waters

over medium tempo backing track

This is a great example displaying the Godfather of the blues' laid-back approach as he effortlessly traverses the fretboard. The licks are common blues vocabulary, but connecting them gracefully as Muddy did is the assignment here. After the quarter step oblique bend and subsequent notes in 12th position, he shifts to 10th position for the greasy, sliding blues lick, and then wraps up by descending to 5th position for a pure minor pentatonic coloring resolving on A.

TRACK 81

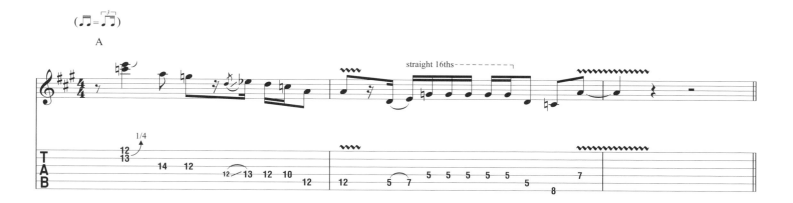

Jeff Beck

over slow tempo backing track

Mr. Beck certainly saved the most challenging licks for last! Here, Jeff plays quick whammy scoops with double stops at the 5th fret while inserting three increasingly deeper whammy bar depressions on the 6th string. The first of the deep growls involves pushing the whammy bar down one octave to a low A, followed by A♭, then finally G.

TRACK 82

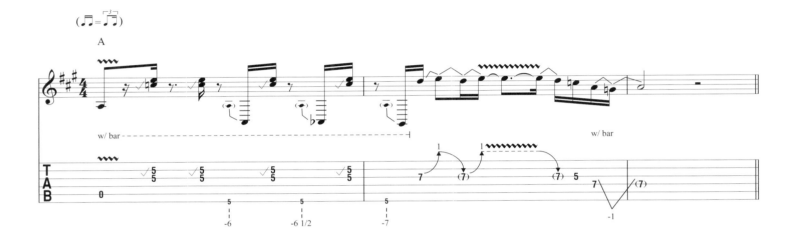

Johnny Winter

over medium tempo backing track

For the conclusion, Johnny slips the C♯ (the major 3rd of the A chord) into an otherwise minor pentatonic lick. The inclusion of the major 3rd in this manner is quite common in blues, provided it's played over the I chord (A in this case). Winter's wonderful sense of syncopation and timing give this phrase its lyrical quality.

TRACK 83

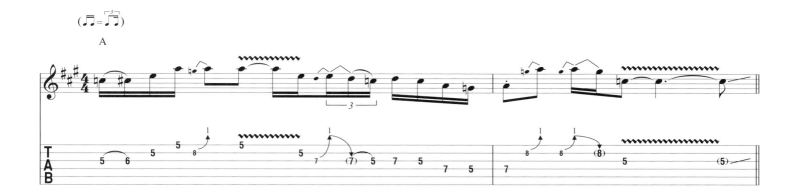

Mark Karan

over slow tempo backing track

More sweet and juicy playing from Mark Karan as he wrap things up. The conclusion of this turnaround forgoes the standard V chord ending in favor of extending the I chord through the 12th measure. Here Mark uses 12th and 5th position boxes from A minor pentatonic, along with a variety of string bending action to color the underlying A chord tonality.

TRACK 84

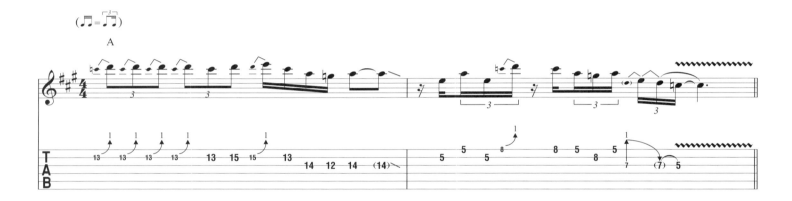

Backing Tracks

Fast Tempo Backing Track

Throughout this book the examples are demonstrated over one of three backing tracks, all looped to repeat. The first backing track is a fast tempo and similar to Cream's live version of "Crossroads." Use this one for all examples directed over the fast tempo backing track.

TRACK 85

Medium Tempo Backing Track

The second backing track is a medium tempo and used for all medium tempo examples. Here the chords are shunned in favor of a riff that implies the chord changes.

Slow Tempo Backing Track

The third backing track is the slowest, and like the second, uses a riff to imply the chord changes, except in the ninth and tenth bars, where the E7#9 and D9 chords are played instead. Also, the typical V chord at the twelfth bar is eschewed in favor of extending the I chord (A) to the finish.

TRACK 87

GUITAR NOTATION LEGEND

Guitar music can be notated three different ways: on a *musical staff*, in *tablature*, and in *rhythm slashes*.

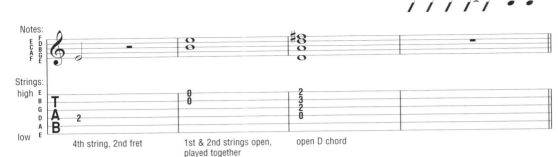

RHYTHM SLASHES are written above the staff. Strum chords in the rhythm indicated. Use the chord diagrams found at the top of the first page of the transcription for the appropriate chord voicings. Round noteheads indicate single notes.

THE MUSICAL STAFF shows pitches and rhythms and is divided by bar lines into measures. Pitches are named after the first seven letters of the alphabet.

TABLATURE graphically represents the guitar fingerboard. Each horizontal line represents a string, and each number represents a fret.

4th string, 2nd fret | 1st & 2nd strings open, played together | open D chord

---

HALF-STEP BEND: Strike the note and bend up 1/2 step.

WHOLE-STEP BEND: Strike the note and bend up one step.

GRACE NOTE BEND: Strike the note and immediately bend up as indicated.

SLIGHT (MICROTONE) BEND: Strike the note and bend up 1/4 step.

BEND AND RELEASE: Strike the note and bend up as indicated, then release back to the original note. Only the first note is struck.

PRE-BEND: Bend the note as indicated, then strike it.

VIBRATO: The string is vibrated by rapidly bending and releasing the note with the fretting hand.

WIDE VIBRATO: The pitch is varied to a greater degree by vibrating with the fretting hand.

HAMMER-ON: Strike the first (lower) note with one finger, then sound the higher note (on the same string) with another finger by fretting it without picking.

PULL-OFF: Place both fingers on the notes to be sounded. Strike the first note and without picking, pull the finger off to sound the second (lower) note.

LEGATO SLIDE: Strike the first note and then slide the same fret-hand finger up or down to the second note. The second note is not struck.

SHIFT SLIDE: Same as legato slide, except the second note is struck.

TRILL: Very rapidly alternate between the notes indicated by continuously hammering on and pulling off.

TAPPING: Hammer ("tap") the fret indicated with the pick-hand index or middle finger and pull off to the note fretted by the fret hand.

NATURAL HARMONIC: Strike the note while the fret-hand lightly touches the string directly over the fret indicated.

PINCH HARMONIC: The note is fretted normally and a harmonic is produced by adding the edge of the thumb or the tip of the index finger of the pick hand to the normal pick attack.

PICK SCRAPE: The edge of the pick is rubbed down (or up) the string, producing a scratchy sound.

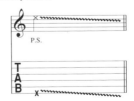

MUFFLED STRINGS: A percussive sound is produced by laying the fret hand across the string(s) without depressing, and striking them with the pick hand.

PALM MUTING: The note is partially muted by the pick hand lightly touching the string(s) just before the bridge.

RAKE: Drag the pick across the strings indicated with a single motion.

TREMOLO PICKING: The note is picked as rapidly and continuously as possible.

VIBRATO BAR DIVE AND RETURN: The pitch of the note or chord is dropped a specified number of steps (in rhythm), then returned to the original pitch.

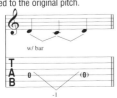

VIBRATO BAR SCOOP: Depress the bar just before striking the note, then quickly release the bar.

VIBRATO BAR DIP: Strike the note and then immediately drop a specified number of steps, then release back to the original pitch.